c/o Library H.Q.
County Hall
Mold CH7 6NW

Gwasanaeth Llyfrgell i Ysgolion
Gogledd-Ddwyrain Cymru

The North-East Wales
Schools Library Service

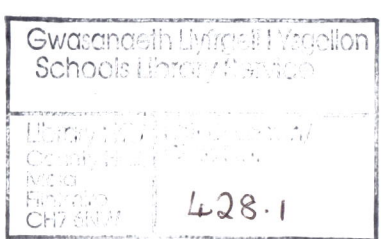
First published in Great Britain by HarperCollins Publishers Ltd in 1997

1 3 5 7 9 10 8 6 4 2
ISBN: 0 00 198256-7

Printed and bound in Hong Kong

butterfly

MY FIRST WORDS

Illustrated by Lynn Breeze

ice cream

keys

hen

flowers

train

house

Collins

An Imprint of HarperCollins*Publishers*

Contents

LOOK AT ME!

eye

face

thumb

neck

chin

back

elbow

bottom

arm

foot

leg

8

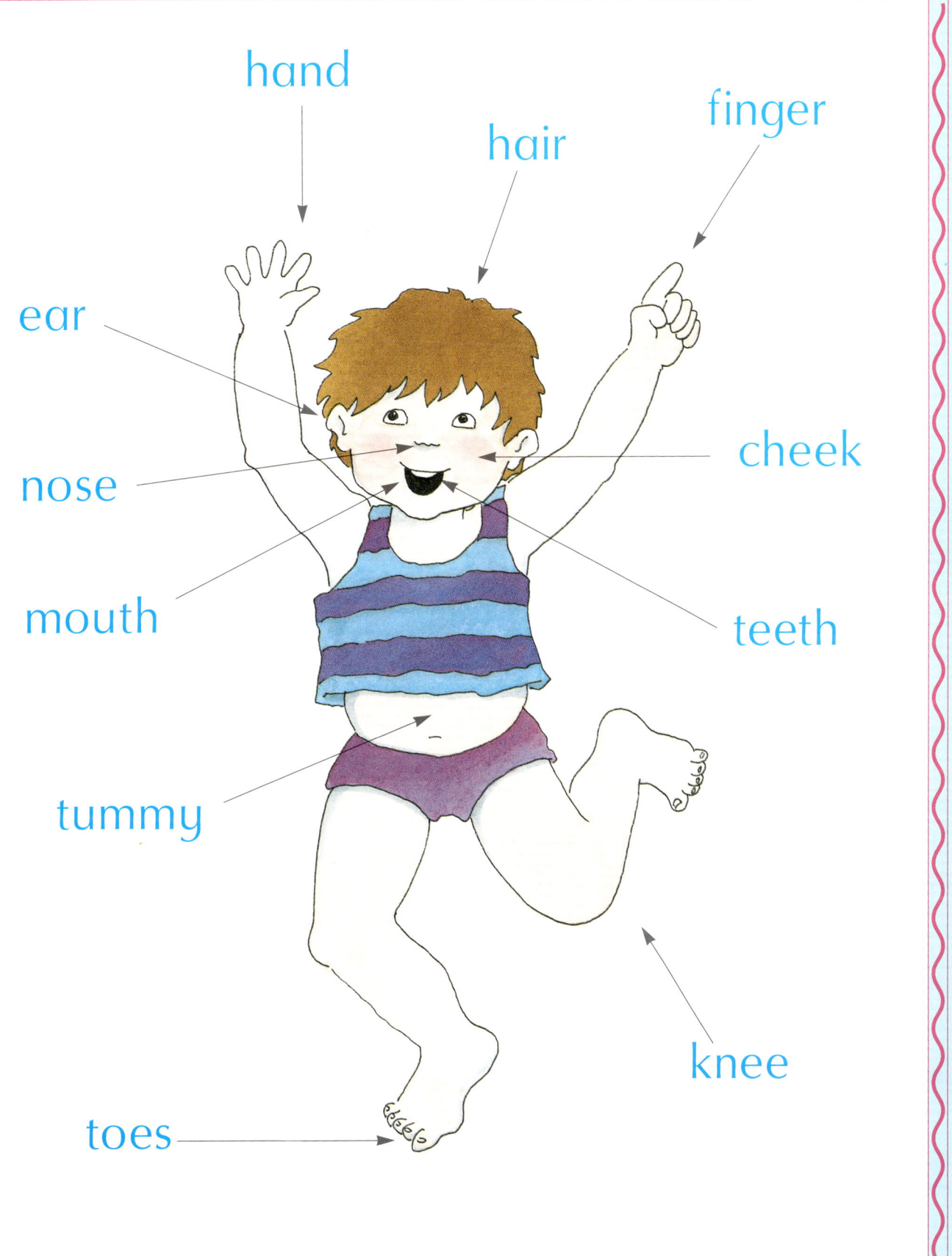

hand

hair

finger

ear

nose

mouth

cheek

teeth

tummy

knee

toes

THINGS TO WEAR

jeans

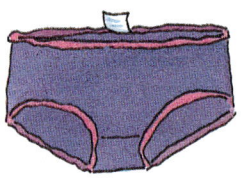
pants

shirt

wellingtons

dress

shoes

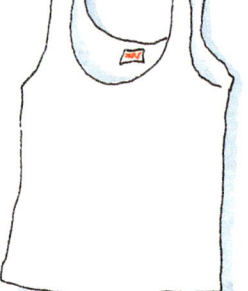

vest

jumper

 T-shirt

hat

 shorts

socks

coat

skirt

dungarees

HOW'S THE WEATHER?

rainy

snowy

windy

sunny

TOYS AND GAMES

crayons

blocks

puppet

pram

telephone

paints

teddy

doll

balloon

jigsaw

jack-in-the-box

skipping rope

COLOURS ARE FUN!

purple

blue

grey

red

white

brown

black

pink

orange

green

yellow

FOOD AND DRINK

bread

banana

sausage

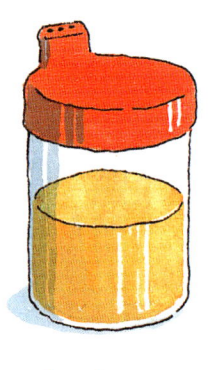

juice

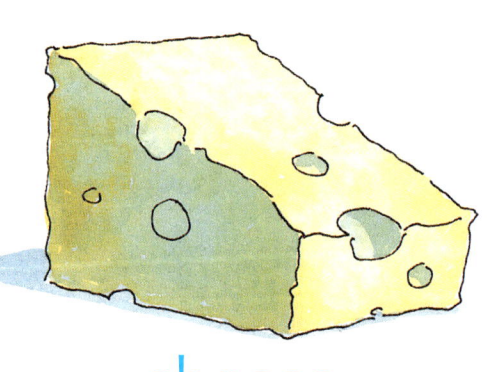

cheese

butter

pie

biscuit

crisps

pasta

sandwich

chocolate

apple

AROUND THE HOUSE

window

door

sofa

newspaper

cupboard

television

iron

lamp

plant

armchair

table

21

IN THE KITCHEN

fork

jug

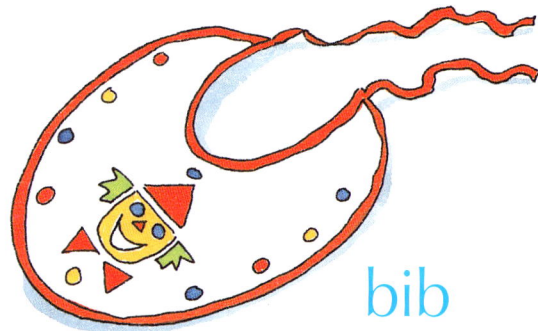
bib

cup and saucer

colander

knife

pan

tea towel

plate

mug

egg cup

spoon

glass

teapot

IN THE BEDROOM

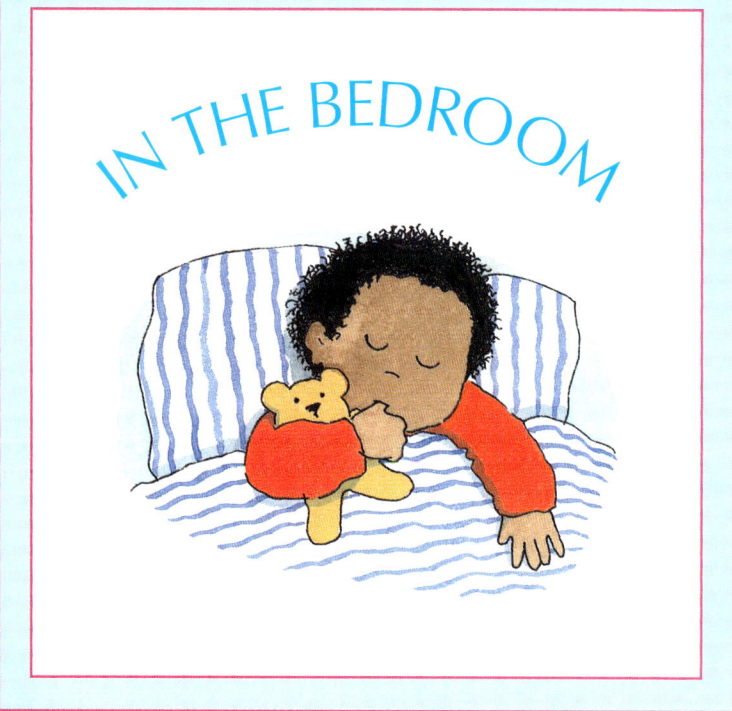

dressing gown

pillow

tissues

comb

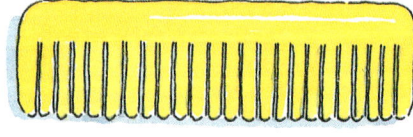

bed

hot-water bottle

pyjamas

clock

duvet

nightie

slippers

hairbrush

IN THE BATHROOM

bath book

mirror

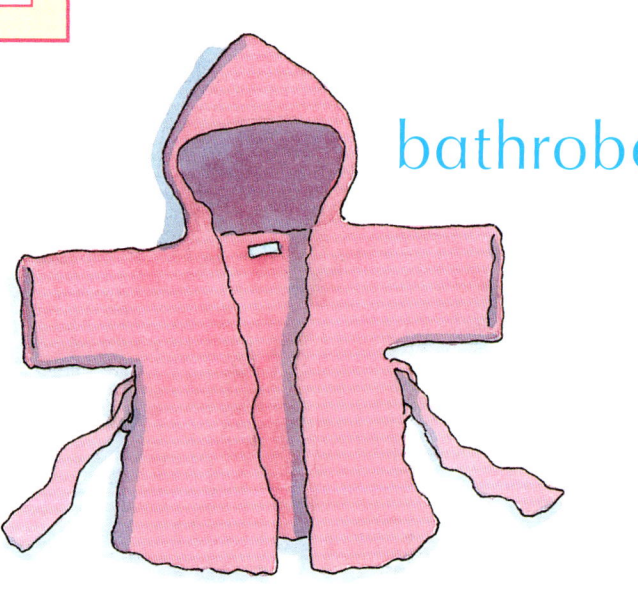

bathrobe

loo roll

cotton wool

talcum powder

toothpaste

shampoo

nappy

potty

duck

toothbrush

sponge

IN THE GARDEN

plant pot

string

snail

leaf

wheelbarrow

worm

watering can

seeds

trowel

bee

garden fork

caterpillar

GOING SHOPPING

washing powder

fish

carrots

tomato

bag

yoghurt

pepper

peas

potatoes

cereal

cake

onions

purse

milk

IN THE PARK

squirrel

tree trunk

swan

swing

lolly

picnic

seesaw

kite

bird

slide

football

ON THE FARM

dog

chick

tractor

wheat

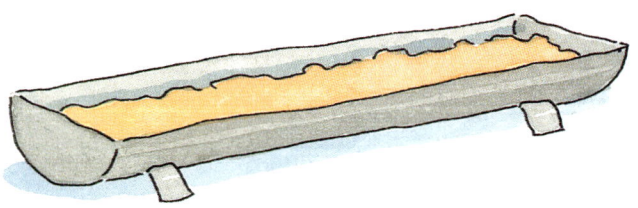

trough

pig

hay bale

goose

lamb

sheep

cow

cockerel

AT THE SEASIDE

shell

crab

ball

bucket

sand castle

seaweed

trunks

pebbles

swimsuit

sunhat

towel

sunglasses

rubber ring

sun block

spade

ANIMALS AND BIRDS

rabbit

owl

parrot

frog

goat

puppy

horse

tortoise

snake

monkey

cat

TRANSPORT

car

boat

bus

bicycle

lorry

skateboard

motorbike

aeroplane

helicopter

tricycle

roller skates

van

I CAN COUNT!

1

one

2

two

3
three

4

four

5

five

6  six

7  seven

8  eight

9  nine

10  ten

Index